JANET DENISON

OUR
Christmas
STORIES

26 REFLECTIONS TO ENRICH YOUR CHRISTMAS SEASON

TABLE OF CONTENTS

PREFACE

I was watching *Reunited at Christmas,* a *Hallmark Channel* Christmas movie, when I heard a message that became the inspiration for this year's Advent book. The movie was about a family that needed healing after their mother and grandmother had passed away.

Before her passing, Grandma had written a letter to remind her family of an important lesson she had tried to teach them. The matriarch had often said, "Traditions are the stories that families write together." In her letter, she encouraged her family to "keep writing our story."

Each Christmas offers us a chance to add a new chapter to our Christmas stories. While it is a wonderful time to remember the moments that have become our family traditions, it is also an opportunity to "keep writing our stories."

The first Christmas changed the world.

Christmas 2020 concludes a year of changes we couldn't have imagined at this time last year.

Yet, for Christians, our Christmas story remains unchanged: "For unto you is born this day in the city of David a Savior, who is Christ the Lord" (Luke 2:11). The Christmas story is our story, the theme of every holiday season.

Christmas 2020 will be different in many ways yet filled with familiar traditions of years past. It is good to remember that "traditions are the stories that families write together."

Keep writing the stories that others in your lives will remember for the Christmases to come. God has promised to keep writing his story through us.

My thanks to all of you who contributed your thoughts and memories so that I could use them in this year's Advent book. As we read the following stories and messages from others, we are reminded of all that matters most at Christmas. Many of us will also be inspired to include a new tradition in our own Christmas as a result.

May the words of this book enrich your holiday, and may the Lord bless your Christmas season with his holy perfection.

From all of us at Denison Ministries,

Christmas blessings!

CELEBRATING TWO BIRTHS

*"And Joseph also went up from
Galilee, from the town of Nazareth, to
Judea, to the city of David, which is
called Bethlehem, because he was of
the house and lineage of David, to be
registered with Mary, his betrothed, who
was with child."*
—LUKE 2:4–5

Charlie worked in the coal mines in Kentucky. When
his brother passed away at an early age from black
lung disease, the doctor told Charlie, "You take those
kids and move away from here."

There were thirteen children, with one more on the
way.

It was 1935. Because of the Great Depression, few jobs were available. Charlie packed a small truck and drove the family away from all they knew, moving them to Minnesota. He soon found work in a logging camp. They settled into a wooden farmhouse complete with a large kitchen and small outhouse.

On a cold, snowy Christmas Eve, Charlie realized his fourteenth child was about to be born. He sent one of his older children for the midwife while he stayed with his wife, Rosetta. This would be the first birth where Rosetta's own mother would not be her midwife. With a cold Minnesota wind howling outside, Rosetta feared she might have to deliver this one on her own.

Charlie and Rosetta's fourteenth child, a little girl, was born on Christmas Eve. Lorraine was carefully wrapped in blankets and laid on a folded quilt in a dresser drawer.

This year, Lorraine will be eighty-four years old. She is the last surviving child in her family.

Growing up, Christmas Eve always had a double significance for me. We celebrated the birth of two babies each year.

Why?

Because I am Lorraine's middle daughter, Janet.

When he was in town, the circuit-rider preacher used

my grandma's kitchen as his church. My mom grew up knowing that Jesus was her Lord and I did too.

I've often taught that everyone has a *spiritual* family tree. I trace my faith back to the faith of my grandma. She had fourteen children, ten boys and four girls, and was adored by each of them.

I'm sure my grandma was praying to the Lord the night my mom was born. She didn't have her mom with her like the other times, and she would certainly have called out to God for strength and peace.

Imagine how frightened Mary must have felt the day she departed for Bethlehem. She left everything she knew, and everyone she knew, except her husband, Joseph. Imagine how nervous Joseph felt, knowing his young wife was close to delivering the baby—God's baby.

Nothing about their lives had been normal for many months. How many times did they remember and talk together about their angelic visits announcing the news about the baby? Mary was going to deliver God's Son, who they would name Jesus, *Yeshua*, meaning "God is salvation."

In faith and with a great sense of calling, they put their possessions on the donkey and began their journey to Bethlehem.

Mary's faith in God was the same faith my grandma would have turned to for her journey.

The same faith, the same God, the same *Yeshua*.

The Christmas story has always been a story of faith that continues through our own journeys each year.

A SIMPLE FAMILY CHRISTMAS EVE SERVICE

"The Lord is good to those who wait for him, to the soul who seeks him."
—LAMENTATIONS 3:25

A Sunday School teacher passed out a plan for Christmas Eve one year. Martha's family followed that plan every year. She always wanted her children to go to sleep on Christmas Eve remembering that the holiday was, most importantly, about Jesus.

Every Christmas Eve, the family piled into the car to attend their church's Christmas Eve service together. After church, the family returned home to eat a dinner of hot chili and tamales. The kids were allowed to open one gift, usually Christmas PJs. Finally, a plate of cookies and a Coke were set out for Santa.

Then it was time for everyone to settle down for a family Christmas Eve service. It was the *same service* every year, the one recommended by that Sunday School teacher:

Someone would light a Christmas candle and read aloud Luke 2:1–7.

The whole family would sing "Away in A Manger."

Someone would read aloud Luke 2:8–12.

The family would sing "Silent Night."

Someone would read aloud Luke 2:13–14.

The family would sing "Happy Birthday" to Jesus.

They would have a family prayer of thanksgiving around the circle.

Someone would blow out the candle.

Henry Ford reportedly said, "Those who walk with God always reach their destination."

At the beginning of this season, it might be useful to think about all that you would most like to experience this coming Christmas Eve and Christmas Day. What traditions would you like to establish or maintain with your family and friends that will draw them into God's purpose for those days?

This is a perfect time to *take time* and pray about those holy days. The prophet Isaiah wrote, "The Lord waits to be gracious to you, and therefore he exalts himself to show mercy to you. For the Lord is a God of justice; blessed are all those who wait for him" (Isaiah 30:18).

Mary knew that she was walking in obedience to the will of God. When the angel, Gabriel, spoke to her, he said, "Greetings, O favored one, the Lord is with you!" (Luke 1:28). God chose Mary *because* she walked with him.

Mary was going to have a baby, and she had become pregnant before she and Joseph were married. Her culture would have known how to count the weeks too. She could not have known then that there would be a census and that she would safely deliver God's Son among people she did not know.

Mary and Joseph didn't need to know the plan. They just needed to walk with the Author of the plan.

Mary is an example for every generation of God's children. Those who walk with God will be blessed. He has a plan for your Christmas season, and he wants to show you his mercy, his love.

"Blessed are all those who wait for him."

The joy of a Christ-focused Christmas will come to those who wait.

SLOPPY JOES AND PAPER PLATES

*"He will be great and will be called the
Son of the Most High. And the Lord God
will give to him the throne of his father
David, and he will reign over the house of
Jacob forever, and of his kingdom there
will be no end."*
—LUKE 1:32–33

Jane's family moved every year, first with the army
and then because of various job promotions. For
the first twelve Christmas seasons, her family never
felt settled enough in their community to put down
roots. The continuity of the family's Christmas
traditions was made all the more special as a result.

Christmas was celebrated in a different home but
always with familiar joys. Each year, Jane and her
siblings made garlands of popcorn and paper chains

for their tree. They'd unwrap homemade ornaments from years past and share fond memories.

When Christmas Eve rolled around, they'd set up TV trays and eat sloppy joes made with hamburger and cream of mushroom soup because Jane's dad didn't like tomato sauce. There were dill pickles, Lay's potato chips, and chocolate milk. The meal was served using paper plates and cups for easy cleanup after. They ate dinner while watching *Rudolph the Red-Nosed Reindeer*. Later, Mom and Dad would read *The Littlest Angel* to their kids.

Looking back, Jane remembers the ease and simplicity of her childhood Christmas compared with the elaborate meals and decorations that are popular today. Times change, and eventually can change again. In recent years, Jane has chosen to return to her childhood values. She works to celebrate the holiday with simplicity, keeping it *simply focused* on Christ.

Chances are, Jane's mom didn't prepare her mushroom soup and sloppy joe dinner to provide a special memory or teach a priority—but it did. When you think back to your childhood memories, do you remember something elaborate or a simple joy?

Most of us will spend this year's Christmas closer to home. It's surprising how much of our normal Christmas celebrations involved large crowds. Are you missing the crowded malls with different school choirs singing carols? Is your December calendar page uncharacteristically empty? Have your travel plans changed, or even been eliminated?

Should we just "get through" this Christmas or does God have a different plan?

Simplicity has never defined Christmas as much as it will this year. We can all "just get through" this holiday or we can embrace its uniqueness.

What will make this year memorable?

Will it be a cold walk around the neighborhood with kids and grandkids to enjoy the lights? Will it be opening gifts with each other via computer screens? Will it be reading a Christmas story together with FaceTime?

How many simple joys can you include in this year's Christmas season? You may be as surprised as Jane's mom could have been to discover it was the simplicity of the holiday that provided the "pleasant."

Simplicity best describes the surroundings Jesus chose to make his first home. It was a cave in a small town that had been crowded with travelers. It was just Mary and Joseph's arms that held him as he wore swaddling cloth. His bed was a manger, the place animals would use to feed.

Jesus chose to be born into simplicity. This is one of the *only* Christmases we will ever experience when we can choose the same.

The Psalmist wrote, "Be still, and know that I am God. I will be exalted among the nations, I will be exalted in the earth!" (Psalm 46:10). Now, hear those words spoken to you by Jesus for this year's Christmas.

The crowded, busy Christmases will return. But this year we can be still and remember that the baby, born into quiet simplicity was, and still is, God.

That is the simple, eternal truth of Christmas.

LIGHTING THE LUMINARIAS

"Again Jesus spoke to them saying, 'I am the light of the world. Whoever follows me will not walk in darkness, but will have the light of life.'"
—JOHN 8:12

Cindy spent her high school years in a wonderful neighborhood near St. Louis. On Christmas Eve and Christmas night, Cindy's street provided a favorite Christmas moment for her community.

One neighbor was chosen each year to gather the supplies needed (paper sacks, sand, and candles) to make hundreds of luminarias. Each family would be responsible for making enough lanterns to cover the sidewalk in front of their house. For most Christmas seasons, snow was on the ground, which helped reflect the light. Other families from the community would drive past and wave, enjoying the beautiful scene, making it part of their Christmas celebrations.

Cindy remembers helping light the luminarias and then her family would join the others as they walked along the street, wishing one another a Merry Christmas and enjoying the quiet beauty and significance of their decorations.

Luminarias are a Christmas tradition of Latin culture and were intended to signify the encouraging of the Spirit of the Christ child to enter one's home. Luminarias are just paper sacks filled with sand and a small candle. One alone doesn't give off very much light, but, when hundreds are combined, they create a pathway for others.

The magi followed the light of a star, which led them to Jesus. Matthew 2:1–2 says, "Now after Jesus was born in Bethlehem of Judea in the days of Herod the king, behold, wise men from the east came to Jerusalem, saying, 'Where is he who has been born king of the Jews? For we saw his star when it rose and have come to worship him.'" Why was Matthew the only gospel author to include the story of the magi?

Matthew knew that his Jewish readers would know about the tragic deaths of the babies in Bethlehem after the magi had come. In this period of history, the Jewish people would have likely been the *only* people group that would have known about it. The deaths of those babies caused great grief in the region, and the news would have been shared among the people of the Jewish nation.

Matthew wrote his gospel to lead the Jewish people to understand and accept that Jesus was their long-awaited Messiah. That's why Matthew began with a lengthy genealogy, proving that Jesus was of the lineage of King David, and therefore fulfilling Old Testament prophecies. The gospel of Matthew is often called the "bridge" between the Old Testament and the New.

Every Christmas, there are people who are led to a nativity set or church service who struggle to understand and believe that Jesus is their Savior. They wonder why we believe and even wish they *could* believe. As Christians, we share the same task Matthew had when he wrote his gospel. We are called to say what a person needs to hear so they can come to a place of conviction and belief in Jesus as their Messiah.

Matthew is also the gospel writer who tells us about Zechariah. Zechariah was serving in the temple when the angel Gabriel appeared to him and told him that he and his wife would have a son. Elizabeth had been unable to conceive, and now they were advanced in years, so Zechariah had expressed his doubts to Gabriel. Gabriel replied, "I am Gabriel. I stand in the presence of God, and I was sent to speak to you and bring you this good news. And behold, you will be silent and unable to speak until the day that these things take place, because you did not believe in my words, which will be fulfilled in their time" (Luke 1:19–20).

17

Everything the angel Gabriel spoke came to pass. This is another story that would have been known only to the Jewish people. Zechariah and Elizabeth named their son John, whom we know as John the Baptist. Their son was called to "prepare the way" for the Messiah. Many of the early disciples of Christ were followers of John.

For every Christian who wants to encourage others to understand the biblical purpose of Christmas, we have knowledge that can "light the way" so that the "Christ child" will be welcomed.

We are called to help others understand *Christ*mas.

NO TACKLING THE CENTER

"May the God of hope fill you with all joy and peace in believing, so that by the power of the Holy Spirit you may abound in hope."
—ROMANS 15:13

Marty's grandma, known as Granny Truelove, had six children. The family farm had been home to several generations and was the traditional gathering place for Christmas Day. When Christmas Day arrived, seven women brought loads of prepared food and then continued cooking after arriving. Marty remembers the amazing smells that filled the home that day. There was no room inside for all the desserts, so those dishes were placed on several long tables in the garage.

There was a big Christmas tree in the den, and the gifts filled the floor around the tree and flowed into the next room. After lunch had been eaten and the gifts had been opened, the family would go out into the field across the road for a football game. Marty always had to play center, and everyone was issued a "no tackling the center" warning because she was the *only girl cousin* in the game!

Marty remembers it was always cold, but nobody cared. That football game was tradition. She said, "The love of and for family overcame all!"

Christmas is often marked by a sense of *abundance.* The stores are never more crowded than in December. The calendar is usually full. There is more cooking, more family, more music, and more and more and more. Abundance is wonderful when there is abundant joy and abundant love.

How do we look for abundance in a Christmas marked by simplicity?

We can look for those things that were abundant in the first Christmas.

The shepherds were in the fields when the skies were filled with abundance. The Bible says, "An angel of the Lord appeared to them, and the glory of the Lord shone around them" (Luke 2:9). There was an abundance of God's glory.

When Mary and Joseph arrived in Bethlehem, there was no room for them in the inn. There was an abundance of people who didn't realize that the most important moment in history was occurring in their midst. There was an abundance of distraction.

When the magi arrived, the gifts they'd brought had abundant value. Those gifts would enable Joseph to keep his wife and son safe in Egypt when they were forced to flee from Herod.

What is abundant this year?

Many have lost jobs, lost family members, lost in an election, or simply lost hope. They wouldn't describe this past year as a year of *abundance*—at least not an abundance of what they would have wanted.

Mary and Joseph had been through a lot. They'd been engaged, then discouraged, then joyful, then married. They'd made a difficult trip and then were given a cave in which to make their home and their nursery. And then they'd been given the Son of God to raise. They had almost nothing in terms of material prosperity, but they held the most precious gift ever given.

You may or may not have material prosperity this year, but that doesn't define abundance for a Christian anyway. Our abundance is the hope of Christmas. Jesus is born and we have a Savior.

We are *abundantly* blessed.

THREE SPECIAL GIFTS

"Worthy are you, our Lord and God, to receive glory and honor and power, for you created all things, and by your will they existed and were created."
—REVELATION 4:11

A friend shared a tradition with Charlyn that has been part of their family's Christmas celebration for almost thirty years. When her children were very young, Charlyn struggled with the increasing commercialization of Christmas. So, when her kids were old enough to understand, she adjusted their expectations of Christmas.

Charlyn taught her children to ask for three special gifts from Santa because the baby Jesus had received three special gifts from the wise men. Making that connection helped eliminate some of the crazy frenzy of shopping and helped her kids learn to be thoughtful about their choices.

Even though Charlyn's children are adults now, they still ask "Santa" for three gifts each Christmas. It is a wonderful way to connect gift-giving to the reason we give gifts at Christmastime. When used in the Bible, the number three signifies a perfect or complete amount.

Most nativity sets have three wise men. In fact, we sing a hymn titled "We Three Kings." The truth is, there were probably *many* people who followed the star and traveled from the east to find the king. The prophet Daniel was considered a wise man, even by those who had taken him captive to Babylon. It was his wisdom and faith that had been proven true to the Babylonian king. Therefore, it is likely that Daniel had taught the prophecies that the magi—all from the regions of that area—had studied.

Daniel taught that, one day, God would send his Messiah and this Messiah would be a King. The book of Daniel tells us, "And to him was given dominion and glory and a kingdom, that all the peoples, nations, and languages should serve him; his dominion is an everlasting dominion, which shall not pass away, and his kingdom one that shall not be destroyed" (Daniel 7:14).

The magi had gone to see Herod, saying, "Where is he who has been born king of the Jews? For we saw his star when it rose and have come to worship him" (Matthew 2:2).

Herod's advisors had told them about Micah's prophecy that the Messiah would be born in Bethlehem. So the magi left to go in search of "the king."

In this culture, the magi would have traveled as a large group, with many camels and servants. Their arrival would have caused a stir at Herod's palace, and especially in the small village of Bethlehem. The magi found the home they had been searching for and "going into the house, they saw the child with Mary his mother, and they fell down and worshiped him. Then, opening their treasures, they offered him gifts, gold and frankincense and myrrh" (Matthew 2:11).

There have been studies done on the significance of the gifts presented to Jesus, but those thoughts can actually detract from the more important point. The wise men, having traveled by camel and by foot, across deserts and difficult terrain, *found the king* they had studied and learned about. When they saw Jesus, who was a young toddler at the time, the magi "fell down and worshiped him." Only *after* that did they open their treasures.

All of us can get caught up in the giving of gifts at Christmas. We love our family and friends, and we wish we could give them something *perfect* that they will value. It might help to remember that the *only perfect* gift of Christmas is Jesus. Whatever else we give, we should include Jesus in our giving.

And wise people still give what the wise people gave Jesus. We can give him the honor, glory, and worship the King deserves. Those are the three gifts we can present to Jesus this Christmas.

HELP IN HARD TIMES

*"Give, and it will be given to you. Good
measure, pressed down shaken together,
running over, will be put into your lap.
For with the measure you use it will be
measured back to you."*
—LUKE 6:38

Sarah's husband was a supervisor at a major oil
company. When the company offered an early
retirement option, it was just too good to pass up. He
was only fifty-nine years old, and their children were
out of college and working.

After a lot of thought and prayer, Sarah and her
husband jumped at the chance to fully enjoy the
next season of their lives. They had a group of close
friends at their church, First Baptist Port Arthur, who
loved to travel, and they spent many years seeing the
country and the world with their best friends.

In November of 1998, Sarah's husband grew very ill. He was treated at a local hospital but didn't improve. They saw a specialist who diagnosed him with a noncancerous cyst on his pancreas. The good news was that removing the cyst would allow him a full recovery. The bad news was that they would be spending the Christmas holiday in the hospital.

The surgery went well. The doctor told them they should be able to go home in just a few days. Sarah and her husband spent Christmas Eve watching holiday programs filled with their favorite Christmas music. It was during one of those programs that Sarah's husband began to talk incoherently and kept trying to get out of the bed. Sarah quickly rang for the nurse, and it was decided that he needed to go back to the ICU.

They lifted him to the carrier. Sarah kissed him and said, "I love you."

He responded, "I love you too."

Sarah dozed off and on the rest of that night and was awakened at six a.m. on Christmas morning. The hospital's chaplain had come to tell her that her husband had died peacefully during the night.

Even in her state of shock, Sarah had to function. She called her children on Christmas morning to tell them that their daddy had died. The only thought that brought them peace was the knowledge that he was in heaven, spending Christmas with his Savior.

But Sarah didn't want to tell her story, to share the sadness of that Christmas Day. The reason that Christmas 1998 is her most important is because of what happened *after* leaving the hospital.

Sarah's husband was a deacon in their church. A deacon-brother, one of their best friends, had volunteered to drive Sarah and her husband to Houston for the surgery. Another couple, who were also close friends, would come back and get them when it was time to come home.

Soon after Sarah had finished packing and making all the necessary arrangements that fateful Christmas morning, she looked up to see her close friends who had rushed to Houston on Christmas Day. When Sarah later arrived home, she saw several cars parked on the street.

Good friends had come to her house with food. They then commenced cleaning the house, using their Christmas afternoon to make sure Sarah knew she was loved and cared for. Christmas 1998 will always be a difficult memory because that was the day Sarah lost her husband. But that Christmas is a significant memory because it is also a reminder of the value of Christian friendship.

Those friends enabled Sarah to endure the pain and know she was greatly loved. She credits their friendship and prayers for carrying her through the difficult days that followed. Because of their sacrificial love, Christmas is still a day to celebrate the love and joy of Christ and the provision of Christmas.

Sarah's story is a wonderful reminder to each of us.

We all know someone who needs friendship this holiday season, and they shouldn't have to ask for it.

What can we simply do or give that will build them up, provide them comfort, or bless their life?

Whom is God calling us to befriend this Christmas?

Let's ask God because, chances are, those friends won't ask us for what they need.

Mary and Joseph asked for a room, but there wasn't space for them. The innkeeper gave them a stable. The wise men didn't ask the young couple if they could give. They just opened their treasure and gave. We have their stories in our Bibles for a reason.

Whom will be blessed this Christmas because of those examples?

PIZZA AT THE HOSPITAL

"Even the Spirit of truth, whom the world cannot receive, because it neither sees him nor knows him. You know him, for he dwells with you and will be in you."
—JOHN 14:17

Carrie's daughter, Grace, was born a preemie with multiple birth defects and was only two and a half years old when she was scheduled for her fifth operation. Grace had been in a lot of pain and had stopped walking. A CAT scan revealed her spinal cord was tethering to her spinal column. Her doctor recommended emergency surgery on December 22, 2003.

Precious friends brought over a purple princess Christmas tree with all the trimmings to decorate the hospital room the night before the surgery. Carrie was so grateful to see her little girl's smile.

After the surgery, Grace had to lay flat on her back for two days. The doctor told them the surgery had been extensive, and he couldn't be sure Grace would regain any control of her lower body because of nerve damage.

On Christmas Eve, the hospital allowed Carrie, her husband, and their six-and-a-half-year-old son to spend the night in Grace's hospital room. Her son still describes that night as the best sleepover he ever had. Friends brought a pizza dinner for them and the entire staff of the children's floor. The young family read the Christmas story before they all fell asleep on a blow-up mattress.

Christmas morning Carrie's parents brought breakfast and all the presents from under the tree at home. The young family stayed in their Christmas pjs the entire day and truly enjoyed the blessing of family as they celebrated the birth of Christ. Carrie remembers that time as the most peaceful Christmas she ever had.

Later that afternoon, Grace took her first steps again. By that evening, she was dancing around the room. Carrie describes it as their Christmas miracle.

Grace and her brother are now nineteen and twenty-three, respectively. The family still considers that sweet and simple Christmas as the best one they ever had. It is the Christmas they were focused on a God who gives miracles.

The biblical Christmas story is a story of miracles. But who were the people to experience the *miraculous* during those days?

Of course, Mary and Joseph understood that Jesus' birth was a miracle. Elizabeth and Zechariah knew that Mary's baby was of God. The shepherds experienced the miraculous in the fields, then witnessed a miracle when they came to find the newborn baby. The wise men knew they were in the presence of a King. But, most who lived in those early first-century days missed the miraculous.

For those who knew Mary and Joseph back home, the couple was expecting a child. For those in the inn, there was simply a newborn baby crying in the stable. The shepherds in other fields had a good night's sleep and woke to tend to their sheep for another day. *Most* people missed the miracle of Christ's birth.

Frederick Buechner wrote, "The sacred moments, the moments of a miracle, are often the everyday moments, the moments which, if we do not look with more than our eyes or listen with more that our ears reveal only a gardener, a stranger coming down the road behind us, a meal like any other meal. But if we look with our hearts, if we listen with all our being and imagination, what we may see is Jesus himself."

Buechner also said, "It is not the objective proof of God's existence that we want but . . . the experience of God's presence. That is the miracle we are really after. And that is also, I think, the miracle that we really get."

Most people missed the miracle of Christmas. Most people still do.

The babe of Bethlehem is the King who saves our souls. That King is the Holy Spirit who has chosen to indwell the life of every believer.

The baby Mary held in her arms is the Spirit which lives in us. He is present, and that is our proof that Christmas is still a miracle today.

Let's not miss the miracle of Christmas.

A WONDERFUL CHURCH FAMILY

*"Whoever brings blessing will be enriched,
and one who waters will himself be
watered."*
—PROVERBS 11:25

Elsa was born in Cuba. Her family became refugees when she was just a young girl. Elsa married a doctor and was soon raising four children on a family farm in East Texas.

Without warning on December 3, 1973, Elsa suddenly became a widow.

She was left with the tasks of closing her husband's medical practice and selling the farm, as well as many other details, while managing the grief she and her four children were experiencing.

Elsa had no family in town, nor any family in Texas. But she did have her wonderful church family. Two women arrived at her home and said, "We are in charge of Christmas. Give us your children's Santa lists. No questions asked!"

Elsa handed the ladies the list and a blank check (that was never used).

By December 15, her home had a fully decorated Christmas tree with wrapped presents lying underneath. One friend surveyed the room and said, "There aren't enough packages under the tree!" Santa came early that year, and soon the room was filled with gifts.

Elsa will always be grateful to Sally and Jan, who provided a joy-filled Christmas holiday for her grieving family. There will never be a Christmas that she doesn't remember and thank the Lord for the gift of their friendship and compassion.

God created us to need other people. No one is exempt from the challenges that come from living on this side of heaven.

This year, all of us know a family that will struggle to make Christmas what they wish it could be. In fact, there are more this year than most. Sometimes the needs can seem overwhelming, but God didn't call us to meet everyone's needs. He calls us to meet *someone's* need.

Mary was pregnant and people would have presumed sin. They couldn't know that her son was the long-awaited Messiah, created by God's Holy Spirit. There are so many details surrounding the birth of Christ that we cannot know, but the Lord made certain we would know about Mary's trip to see Elizabeth.

Scripture says, "When Elizabeth heard the greeting of Mary, the baby leaped in her womb. And Elizabeth was filled with the Holy Spirit, and she exclaimed with a loud cry, 'Blessed are you among women, and blessed is the fruit of your womb!'" (Luke 1:41–42).

Elizabeth, pregnant with her own son, was Spirit-filled and rejoiced with Mary. God, through his Holy Spirit, provided Mary the encouragement and help she needed. Someone else *understood*.

There might be gifts to purchase and give that are for children we will never see or know this side of heaven. The Holy Spirit can guide us to know how to give. There will also be moments of ministry that the Holy Spirit will prompt, e.g., a card or an email to someone you haven't spoken to for years but whom the Lord has placed on your heart.

For some, this Christmas will be a holiday they want to wish away because it is painful. The Holy Spirit can give you God's joy to share. Even in difficult circumstances, there can be Christmas joy.

Through Elizabeth, the Holy Spirit brought Mary the joy she needed. Mary's praise to God, known as the Magnificat, begins, "My soul magnifies the Lord, and my spirit rejoices in God my Savior" (Luke 1:46–47).

Elizabeth's greeting was Spirit-led and therefore ministered to both women. They were blessed by God, and that was joy. The Lord made certain we would have their examples in our Christmas story. Each year, the book of Luke reminds us that the Holy Spirit can work through our lives to bless others.

We were created to need others and then gifted by the Holy Spirit to meet others' needs. That is our Christmas joy.

THE TRAVELING NATIVITY

*"In the same way, let your light shine
before others, so that they may see your
good works and give glory to your Father
who is in heaven."*
—MATTHEW 5:16

Jeannine had four young children, and she wanted them to understand the true meaning of Christmas. The very first decoration in their home each Christmas was the nativity set, or, more accurately, a partial nativity set.

Jeannine would put their crèche out, but she kept most of it empty. There was only the straw and an empty manger. The pieces to the nativity were scattered throughout the house. The cows and sheep were in the room with the small stable. Mary and Joseph were in another room with the donkey nearby. The shepherds and the sheep were placed in a quiet room, away from everything else. The wise men were put in a spot farthest away from the stable.

As the Christmas holiday progressed, the pieces began to *travel*, inching closer to the stable each day. Their journey helped the family experience the Advent season in a unique and memorable way. Jeannine had the opportunity to share the biblical story of Christmas with her children in a way they were sure to understand and *remember*.

The last thing Jeannine did on Christmas Eve was place the baby Jesus in the manger. Amazingly, the first thing her children did each Christmas Day was run to see if Jesus had been *born*. It was a great reminder to her whole family of the true celebration for the day.

The nativity set was the last decoration Jeannine put away each year. The three kings didn't find Jesus until later. The *gift* of Christmas continued even after the holiday.

There are so many creative ways to share the Christmas story with our families and others. Imagine walking into Jeannine's home and noticing the different pieces of her nativity set scattered throughout her home. Often, our best witness has no words.

People can learn the Christmas story by reading our lives, by seeing our priorities, and by noticing our joy. Kindness doesn't require shopping, wrapping, or sending, yet it is a wonderful gift to give. Most people just want to know you care. Many can't imagine that the God who created the world did so for them.

Much of the time, our witness has no words but speaks loudly to those around us. And people *are* listening.

Jeannine may never know who thought about the true meaning of Christmas because of her traveling nativity. At a very young age, I imagine her children would have been able to tell the biblical Christmas story to their friends.

Some of our best lessons are shared with people we will never meet in this lifetime. But imagine meeting them in heaven one day and hearing them say, "Remember when you . . . ."

If you are like me, you became interested in Christ when Christians became interesting. Most people are drawn to the Lord by those who live for him. Billy Graham said, "We are the Bibles the world is reading. We are the creeds the world is needing. We are the sermons the world is heeding."

There are a lot of ways to share the Christmas story, often without words.

Who will be drawn to the manger on Christmas morning because they were drawn to you?

THEATER NIGHT ON CHRISTMAS EVE

*"And there were in the same country
shepherds abiding in the field, keeping watch
over their flock by night. And, lo, the angel
of the Lord came upon them, and the glory
of the Lord shone round about them."*
—LUKE 2:8–9 KJV

Jonita's family turned their home into a theater for
Christmas Eve. There were four children in the
family: an older daughter, twin sons, and their baby
sister. Each child played an important role in the
Christmas play according to their age or their choice
of role for that year.

Each child was draped in whatever fabric remnants
that could be scrounged from the remnant closet.
Halos were crafted from tinsel garland and anything

else that sparkled. A manger was fashioned out of whatever was handy, and the youngest child would be wrapped up and put inside. Someone usually chose to be Mary, dressed in blue and white.

After everyone had created their costume, the Christmas story would be read, and the characters came to life as the story was acted out. Sometimes, hymns were played and sung as part of the script. (After all, everyone loves a great musical performance!)

Each year, the characters changed as the children grew. As a result, the Christmas story was presented in a new and unique way each year.

When the play was over, the family would enjoy dinner and open one small gift. Then everyone would go to bed, looking forward to Christmas Day and knowing why the holiday was special.

Sometimes people think of the Christmas story as simply a *story*. To many people, Mary, Joseph, the shepherds, etc. were just actors on a stage. The story of Jesus can be read like the story of Santa.

How do we make sure the world understands that the biblical story of Christmas is *the* Christmas story?

Jonita's children knew they were representing real people, with real lives, and portraying real events. They will walk by a nativity set and know the baby inside was God's son, their Messiah. Jonita wanted the Christmas story to be real to them.

We live in a culture that has placed all religions in a box marked: "Choose what you would like—and then keep it to yourself," especially if you are a Christian. The irony is that almost all of them celebrate *Christ*mas.

Maybe the best thing all of us can do is realize that we *are* actors on a stage *and* we have an audience. We need to present the Christmas story to the world as an historical event.

In fact, it was the event that most changed history. We are in a large, worldwide *cast*. There are 2.3 billion of us who believe that "God so loved the world, that he gave his only Son, that whoever believes in him will have everlasting life" (John 3:16).

Most of us will hear the Christmas story from the book of Luke. The reason that the first two chapters of Luke are most often used to tell the Christmas story is that Luke was a historian and details mattered. Theologians believe Luke interviewed Mary while in Ephesus, and that is when he learned the information his gospel reveals.

The Christmas story from the book of Luke is familiar to each of us. Most of us remember watching Linus, holding his blue blanket, and reciting it to the school auditorium. Charles Schultz's Christmas cartoon is an annual tradition still. In his cartoon, Linus' performance included telling the biblical text of Luke. After the room heard those words, the whole room changed from chaos to quiet. There is great power in biblical truth. If Linus could quiet Lucy and Charlie with God's words, we can quiet our culture too.

Our Christmas story is historical truth. We can share it with confidence. Those words have changed people's lives for thousands of years and will continue to do so until time is complete.

Linus told Charlie Brown, "I can tell you what Christmas is all about."

We can tell our culture too.

A DIFFERENT CHURCH EACH DAWN

"Blessed are the peacemakers, for they shall be called sons of God."
—MATTHEW 5:9

Cristina grew up in the Catholic faith and has fond memories of an early 4 a.m. Mass she attended for nine consecutive days leading up to Christmas Eve. The churches where she grew up were decorated with colorful Filipino lanterns called *parol*, and each had a large nativity scene on display. Her church youth group would visit a different church each dawn, experience the Mass, and then enjoy the different Christmas decorations at each church.

For Cristina, Christmas wasn't about the parties and the gift-giving as much as it was a *celebration* of the holy season. Her grandparents had migrated to the

Philippines to escape communism. Her family had adapted to some of the Filipino traditions but didn't celebrate Christmas like most of their neighbors. For example, Cristina didn't grow up believing in Santa.

When Cristina met and married her husband, Russell, Christmas traditions became a *negotiation*. How would they celebrate? Would they teach their child about Santa, as Russell had enjoyed, or would they do something different?

When their daughter was old enough to understand that "Santa" brought presents, they discussed what they should do. They didn't want their daughter to miss out, but, at the same time, they didn't want her to believe that Santa was the most important part of Christmas either.

So they created a new tradition, one they still enjoy today.

Each Christmas morning, a gift awaits their daughter with a tag that says, "From Jesus." They wanted her to believe that Jesus gives the best gifts. In fact, they taught her that "all gifts," even those presents people believe are from Santa, are really from God anyway.

Even though she is a young woman today, her daughter has said that her favorite thing about Christmas each year is her "Jesus gift." Her favorite Jesus gift was a mission trip to Romania that her parents enabled her to take.

Cristina hopes that her daughter will want to continue their family's "Jesus gift" tradition one day with her own children.

If you had one wish for your "Jesus gift," what would it be?

There are a lot of spoofs done of beauty pageant contestants who answer a question like that with the words, "World peace." But, world peace is the main point of the Christmas story.

The angel told the shepherds they would find the baby wrapped in swaddling clothes, lying in a manger. Then the heavens opened up, "and suddenly there was with the angel a multitude of the heavenly host praising God and saying, 'Glory to God in the highest, and on earth peace among those with whom he is pleased!'" (Luke 2:13–14).

Let's remember what Linus from *Peanuts* knew. We know what Christmas is "all about." Let's share the peace of God and the peace of Christmas today.

That would be a "Jesus gift" to give.

SANTA BROUGHT THE TREE

"Therefore the Lord himself will give you a sign. Behold, the virgin shall conceive and bear a son, and shall call his name Immanuel."
—ISAIAH 7:14

Barbara's grandfather immigrated to America from Germany at the age of eighteen and eventually married. Barbara's dad was the youngest of nine children, and he always loved everything about Christmas.

Many of the traditions and celebrations we think of as our own were actually brought to our country by immigrants. Wooden nativity sets, many of our Christmas carols, the Advent wreath, and the Advent calendar all have their origins in the European celebrations of Christmas.

Barbara's family embraced their new country but celebrated Christmas with their early traditions. Their home was fully decorated, inside and out. One of their German traditions was to have Santa Claus bring the tree and all the gifts on the night of Christmas Eve.

Barbara's father raised his children with those traditions. He loved Christmas, but he taught his children that the most important tradition of the holiday was the celebration of Jesus' birth. Barbara and her siblings never saw what "Santa brought" on Christmas morning until after they got home from church. She remembers it was hard to sit still for those early Christmas services, but the "magic" of Christmas was never confused with the miracle of Jesus' birth.

Barbara didn't continue the German tradition of Santa Claus bringing the tree and the gifts with her children and grandchildren. But, she did make sure to continue to focus their Christmas celebration on the miracle of Jesus' birthday rather than the magic of Santa Claus.

It has always been difficult to balance the world's celebration of Christmas with the deeper, true meaning of the biblical story. One of the best ways to help children and others focus the holiday on Christ is to dig into the historical background of our traditions.

Most of us have a Christmas wreath. Traditionally, it is made of evergreen branches in a circular shape to celebrate eternal life. Its candles signify that Jesus is the light of the world.

Holly was used to remind us of the crown of thorns worn by Jesus. Jesus was born at Christmas to become our Savior on Easter.

Mistletoe was an ancient Roman tradition. The Romans believed that broken relationships could be restored while standing underneath mistletoe. Christians adopted the same tradition to teach that Jesus had been born to restore us to a right relationship with God.

Santa Claus comes from a Dutch word, *Sinter Claus*, which is Saint Nicholas in English. The true story of Saint Nicholas will give a perspective to our children (and anyone else) about why and how we can celebrate him at Christmas. He was a giver of gifts because he was a compassionate servant of God's greatest gift, Jesus.

The world puts a different slant on most of our traditions, taking the emphasis *away* from the true symbolism. Knowing the history can help us refocus those traditions on Christ.

The first Christmas wasn't about traditions, decorations, and gifts. It was really only about one thing: the birth of a baby who came to save the world. Every other celebration should help others understand that.

The magic of Christmas *is* the miracle of Christmas.

A LETTER FROM SANTA

"But seek first the kingdom of God and his righteousness, and all these things will be added to you."
—MATTHEW 6:33

Celeste planned ahead for the all-important Christmas card photo with Santa. She bought coordinating outfits for her four young children and scheduled haircuts so they could look just right. Celeste pored over the toy catalogs with her kids so they would have their wish lists ready. (She wanted to make sure she could purchase the toys her kids were going to ask Santa to bring.)

The day for the visit arrived, but things didn't go as planned. Her daughter insisted on wearing her favorite denim jacket over her dress. Her oldest son's dress shoes were way too small. They arrived at the mall mismatched and wearing dirty sneakers.

Undeterred, Celeste rushed them through the mall to see Santa, only to find the wait time was about two hours. Celeste left her husband in line with the baby and tried to figure out how to entertain her other three children until it was time to see Santa.

At one point, Celeste lined her children up in front of a beautifully decorated tree, hoping to snap a Christmas photo. But her youngest son stomped his dirty-sneakered foot and refused to cooperate. In frustration, she told him, "You had better stand still or Santa is going to put you on his naughty list!"

Needless to say, that comment didn't produce the desired effect. No photo-card yet.

Finally, the time arrived to see Santa. Her daughter refused to shed the mismatched denim jacket. Her oldest son asked Santa for nothing on the prearranged gift list. Instead, he requested a toy that was completely sold out and impossible to find. And, her youngest son, fearing he was on the naughty list, refused to sit on Santa's lap, alarmed that he would not be receiving any gifts.

The family returned home exhausted and without the coveted Christmas card photo. That's the evening Celeste reconsidered the direction their holiday had taken. This was not how she wanted her children to *remember* the holiday. She wanted her children to celebrate *Christ*mas.

That year, her children received a letter in the mail from Santa. In the letter, Santa explained that the best gift of Christmas was not a gift he would bring. Santa then quoted John 3:16 and wrote, "My gifts will eventually get old and you will tire of them, but God's gift, Jesus, lasts forever."

Celeste made a few changes in her Christmas priorities and established some family traditions that focused a little more on Jesus and a lot less on things like getting the perfect photo. Christmas became *Christ*mas as a result.

What do you need to take off your Christmas to-do list this week?

As you look at your list, do those things matter, or matter eternally?

It just might free your schedule up to eliminate a few things that don't matter as much as you first thought.

As soon as the angel told the shepherds where to look for the baby Jesus, they left to go find the newborn king in the manger. They had sheep that needed tending. They'd been awake all night and needed rest. But the Messiah had been born and *nothing else* mattered.

The shepherds said to one another, "Let us go over to Bethlehem and see this thing that has happened, which the Lord has made known to us" (Luke 2:15). The shepherds were able to see Jesus.

Chances are, you might have to drop a few things off your to-do list if you want to see Jesus today.

Does anything else matter more?

THE PERFECT TREE

"Beloved, if God so loved us, we also ought to love one another."
—1 JOHN 4:11

Rita grew up in a small town near Houston. Her parents both worked hard to provide for their three daughters. There was money for necessities but not for extras.

Every Christmas, Rita and her sisters would go in search of the perfect Christmas tree on their farm because there wasn't money to buy one of the fancy trees from the store. But searching for their tree became an annual adventure.

They tromped around the farm, looking at all the cedars, hoping to find the *perfect* tree. Several trees were found each year and then rejected for one reason or another. In the end, usually after searching the farm for an hour or more, they would discover the most perfect tree, agreed upon by all.

Rita was a grown woman when she learned that her dad had chosen a tree every winter that would be the next Christmas tree for his family. He spent all year grooming the tree, knowing that he would later guide his children around the farm until they discovered it.

One year, Rita's dad chose a tree that was located near a road. He led his children around the farm, eventually bringing them to a . . . STUMP. Apparently, someone else had thought it would be a *perfect* Christmas tree too!

Looking back, Rita knows that her trees were just common cedar trees, not anything like the trees on the lots in town or the store-bought kind. To many people, her Christmas trees might have looked sad, but they were beautiful to Rita and her sisters.

When Rita thinks about tromping around the farm with her dad to find that tree he had *perfected* for a year, she realizes those thoughts are among her favorite Christmas memories. Those trees were a symbol of her father's love.

"For God so loved the world, that he gave us his only Son that whoever believes in him should not perish but have eternal life" (John 3:16). The perfect Father's love gave the world a perfect gift. Great dads love to provide for their children.

A lot of us grew up having great fathers, but there are always some dads who didn't live up to their task. Truthfully, even great fathers blow it sometimes. Moms too.

But, as we ponder the gifts we want to give this year, none matter as much as the "yearlong" love behind each one. Our kids will probably remember very few of the gifts they received in their lifetime, but they will remember the gifts of time we gave them all year long.

Those are the *perfect* gifts we can give.

Mary and Joseph had nothing to give their newborn son except those things that met his basic needs. The baby Jesus was loved, cared for, and kept safe. When Herod decreed that the babies in Bethlehem under the age of two should be killed, Joseph immediately took his family and fled to Egypt. Scripture says that "an angel of the Lord appeared to Joseph in a dream and said, 'Rise, take the child and his mother, and flee to Egypt, and remain there until I tell you, for Herod is about to search for the child, to destroy him.' And he rose and took the child and his mother by night and departed to Egypt" (Matthew 2:13–14).

Joseph loved his baby and he loved God. He was a good parent too. The best way to love others is to love God and obey his directions.

That is the most *perfect* gift all of us can give, at Christmas and all during the year.

THE FAMILY'S GOLD CROSS AND CHAIN

"For this reason I bow my knees before the Father, from whom every family in heaven and on earth is named."
—EPHESIANS 3:14–15

Jane's family has a Christmas gift that is presented to someone each year. Sharing that gift has become a favorite Christmas moment for her family.

The tradition began the year her Aunt Barbie lost her husband and everyone wanted her to feel loved by her family and by God. They went to the store and bought a gold cross and chain that could be worn by a man or woman. They engraved the word *Family* on its back and placed it in a beautiful wooden box.

Barbie was the first one to receive the cross and the first one to give it away the following year. Each Christmas Eve, the current cross-holder selects the next recipient and explains why they are receiving it for the year. Inside the beautiful wooden box, the cross is accompanied by a plaque that bears the names of the family members who have received the special gift.

Every year, it is an emotional and touching moment for the whole family. The cross has been shared with almost forty people, and Jane hopes that the tradition will be carried on for many generations to come. Christmas has always been a season to celebrate the fact that God created us to be a family.

Jesus could have chosen to step into the world as an adult. Instead, he became a baby in Joseph and Mary's family. Why did Jesus, who had the power to be an earthly King, choose to become a newborn? Why did he choose poverty? Why did he choose a cave and a manger?

Could it be that Jesus chose his circumstances as an example to all of us?

Family is a theme of Scripture from the early moments of Genesis to the last words in Revelation. God created the concept of family and, through faith in his Son, he created his children to be a family of faith. The Bible says, "For all who are led by the Spirit of God are sons of God. For you did not receive the spirit of slavery to fall back into fear, but you have received the Spirit of adoption as sons, by whom we cry 'Abba! Father!' The Spirit himself bears witness with our spirit that we are children of God" (Romans 8:14–16).

God created Adam and Eve and, one generation later, Cain and Abel were fighting. It didn't take long for family issues to enter the story. When God created families, he did so knowing that they would sometimes miss his point. Nevertheless, Jesus chose to be part of a family— a family that would later stand in his way, claiming he was "out of his mind" (Mark 3:21).

The world tells us Christmas is a time for family, and it is. But, mostly, it is a time for our family of faith. Hopefully, our earthly families will celebrate the biblical Christmas story together, but often there are one or two family members who don't share our faith.

Families are imperfect, but we should always remember that Jesus chose to be part of one. We can too. We don't have to change what we believe by faith, but we might have to honor the free will of a family member who chooses not to believe. God created them with free will. Sometimes all we can do is give these family members we love to their Creator. Our job is to love and care about them, not agree with them.

Is it time to forgive, even if you can't accept? Is it time to care about a member of the family, even if they don't seem to care about you? Is it time to love, even when you can't like?

Jesus chose to be part of an imperfect family. We can too. Our perfect Christmases will be spent in heaven. Until then, we can give the gifts that will draw them close to God, and hopefully to the family.

It would be nice to have as many names as possible "engraved" on the list of names of people who knew they were loved.

THE JOY OF BAKING

"Who saved us and called us to a holy calling, not because of our works but because of his own purpose and grace, which he gave us in Christ Jesus before the ages began."
—2 TIMOTHY 1:9

Sheila was a second grader when she received one of her favorite Christmas gifts of all time: a box filled with small bags of cake, muffin, and cookie mixes, accompanied by miniature baking pans.

For days, Sheila prepared and baked each of the mixes in her mom's oven. She still remembers the joy she felt at the finished products! That Christmas gift was the beginning of a lifelong love of baking and cooking for others.

Thirty-plus years later, Sheila, now married with two children, learned that her husband had been called to be the next president of a university. That meant she would need to be . . . a president's wife, a "first lady." While that thought could have brought her a sense of pride, it was difficult for her to feel anything but panic.

Her mind was filled with visions of dignified ladies with beautifully coiffed hair and impeccable clothes. Sheila felt overwhelmed and completely unsuited for the tasks ahead—until she realized that one of her tasks would be cooking, baking, and hosting various events.

God had been equipping Sheila for those tasks since she was eight years old, when she happily began using her favorite Christmas gift. Those thoughts helped provide Sheila the peace she needed for her role ahead. God had been preparing her for her calling throughout her life, gifting her for a role she never could have anticipated.

The angel told Mary, "For nothing will be impossible with God" (Luke 1:37). Those same words encouraged Sheila to know God could enable her for the days ahead. And to think: it all began with a Christmas gift of a child-sized baking set!

The first words the angel spoke to Mary were, "Do not be afraid, Mary, for you have found favor with God" (Luke 1:30). All of us have heard or used the phrase, "The Lord works in mysterious ways." Why does God often call us to do things we perceive to be *outside* of our abilities?

Often, God's calling in our lives is not something we would have chosen or planned. Could it be that God wants us and others to more easily recognize *his work* in the world rather than think we should take credit for those things ourselves?

The Christmas story is a perfect illustration of God's mysterious ways. The angel told Mary, "And behold, you will conceive in your womb and bear a son, and you shall call his name Jesus. He will be great and will be called the Son of the Most High. And the Lord God will give to him the throne of his father David, and he will reign over the house of Jacob forever, and of his kingdom there will be no end" (Luke 1:31–33).

Mary was going to have a son, and he would be the long-awaited Messiah. Mary's first response to God's calling was to say, "How will this be, since I am a virgin?" (Luke 1:34). Mary questioned her calling because it was outside of human possibilities. Quite often, God's calling is exactly that. God wants us to know that his work in our lives is *his doing*, not ours.

How did God's calling work in Mary's life? The same way his calling is fulfilled in our own lives. The angel said, "The Holy Spirit will come upon you, and the power of the Most High will overshadow you" (Luke 1:35). The Holy Spirit has always been the power behind God's work in the world. He still is.

The key to experiencing and fulfilling our calling is to yield to and accept what the Holy Spirit wants to accomplish through our lives. It will likely appear to be *outside* our own abilities. God wants us and others to recognize that it was *his work* in our lives, not our own.

How will the Lord's Holy Spirit "overshadow" you this holiday season to accomplish his work in the world?

When God calls, you can say yes, knowing that "nothing will be impossible with God" (Luke 1:37).

A BICYCLE IN THE BATHTUB

"For by grace you have been saved through faith. And this is not your doing; it is the gift of God."
—EPHESIANS 2:8

Every Christmas, Molli and her brother would receive several gifts under the tree, but there was always one big gift located someplace else. This was the gift they were most excited about because it was the gift they most wanted. Therefore, it became the gift that required a little more work to receive.

Receiving this gift began with a note from their dad that contained a riddle or clue. That note would lead to the next note, which would lead to the next and the next. Molli and her brother spent a good bit of time on Christmas morning running all around the house and the yard, knowing that the coveted gift would be found at the end of the hunt.

One year, there was a bicycle in the bathtub. Another Christmas, there was a special doll, wrapped and waiting in the refrigerator. Gifts were found in the mailbox, the neighbor's porch, and even the clothes dryer.

After Molli married and had children, she continued that favorite tradition with her children, who now continue it with their children. Looking for those "most valued" gifts became the highlight of every Christmas.

It is safe to say that the finest Christmas gift ever given was the gift of God's Son, our Savior. It is baffling that so many in our world settle only for the gifts that are "easy to find." God left us his word so that anyone could follow the clues and find their most coveted gift. The problem is that too few make the "hunt."

Christmas is the perfect time to help people understand that the most important gift of Christmas isn't under their tree. How can we leave them the clues that will help them find Jesus?

Every nativity set is a clue.

Every Christmas card can send a message.

Phone calls, emails, and a thought-filled gift can point people to their need for Jesus.

But, the first step is helping them understand that they have a perfect Christmas gift they need to find.

When did you decide you needed Jesus? What were the clues that led you to your salvation? Chances are, it began with the thought that *everything under the tree* was wonderful, but something was missing. People tend to look for Jesus when they understand how much they need him.

The angels told the shepherds, "For unto you is born this day in the city of David a Savior, who is Christ the Lord" (Luke 2:11). When the glorious angels left, the shepherds' first inclination was to say, "Let us go over to Bethlehem and see this thing that has happened, which the Lord has made known to us" (v. 15). When they understood they had a Savior, they wanted to meet him.

We, like the angels, can be God's messengers this year through the power and leadership of his Holy Spirit. We can tell people how to find Jesus. The first step will probably be helping them to understand that they won't find their most valuable Christmas gift under their tree.

God is their heavenly Father, and he has authored the clues that will guide them to the most perfect gift they will ever receive.

THE GRAHAM-CRACKER CRÈCHE

"To them God chose to make known how great among the Gentiles are the riches of the glory of this mystery, which is Christ in you, the hope of glory."
—COLOSSIANS 1:27

Graylene's mom cherished the beautiful olive wood crèche she had purchased on a trip to Israel. Years later, after Graylene had children of her own, her mom gave her that special crèche to use in her own home.

That nativity set became the first of many that would decorate their home each year. Graylene began collecting crèches from the various places they would travel. Years later, the crèches are displayed throughout the house and represent memories of vacations, mission trips, and other travels.

Now, in addition to her wide array of memorable crèches, she adds another special, albeit temporary, crèche. Each year, she gathers graham crackers, candies, and other treats so that she and her grandchildren can build a crèche of their own. Making the crèche is an annual celebration of the significance of the biblical Christmas story for her family.

Walking through Graylene's home during the holidays is a profound reminder that Christians can be found throughout the world who want to honor and celebrate the birth of Christ.

There is something about "hands-on" work that creates memories. When you remember Christmases of the past, do you think about something your received or something you did?

Most of the Christmas stories I received for this book were about memories of an activity that produced a special memory that person wanted to share.

Graylene's grandchildren can probably speak about every aspect of the Christmas story. They didn't learn that story by reading it first. They built it with their hands. They didn't just hear about the baby in the manger; they held him in their hands. As a result, the story was embedded in their hearts and lives, and every Christmas the nativity displays are symbols of the Christmas story found in God's word. All other *stories* of Christmas stand in the light of *that story.*

Jesus was only a few days old when his parents brought him to the temple in Jerusalem to make the required sacrifice for a newborn son. One of the most precious moments of the Christmas story isn't depicted by a nativity set. Simeon was an elderly man the Bible describes as "righteous and devout" (Luke 2:25) He had been waiting for many years because the Holy Spirit had revealed to him that, one day, he would see the long-awaited Messiah.

Scripture says that Simeon came "in the Spirit" to the temple. "When the parents brought in the child Jesus, to do for him according to the custom of the Law, he took him up in his arms and blessed God" (vv. 27–28).

There are very few moments more precious than holding a newborn infant in our arms, especially when that child is deeply loved. We can take the time today to experience the joy and blessing that Simeon felt when he reached out and received the baby, his Messiah. We have been blessed with that opportunity as well. God has chosen to give us the tangible presence of our Messiah. We hold Jesus too because his Holy Spirit indwells our hearts and lives.

We can make sure the people we love don't just know *about* Jesus but also experience his Presence. No one should just celebrate Jesus during the Christmas season. Everyone can *hold him* in their hearts.

That is the magnificent blessing of his birth and our rebirth.

CAROLS IN THE JAILHOUSE

*"And I heard the voice of the Lord saying,
'Whom shall I send, and who will go for
us?' Then I said, 'Here am I! Send me.'"*
—ISAIAH 6:8

Evelyn was the youngest daughter of two strong,
godly parents. She remembers Christmas 1988 for
two important reasons. Although she didn't know
it at the time, it would be the last Christmas with
her mom. Equally precious was a memory of that
Christmas which involved her dad.

Her dad had pastored in small communities and had
served as a Navy chaplain in World War II and the
Korean War, continuing in the reserves for another
twenty years. Upon his retirement from the ministry,
her parents moved to west Texas.

It was a cold, cloudy Christmas Eve in 1988. Evelyn and her family had traveled from their home in northeast Texas so they could spend the holiday with her folks. Her mom had been struggling with leukemia, and Evelyn was anxious to see her.

When they reached the house, the kids bounded inside, thrilled to be there. Evelyn felt the same way. But her dad stopped her on the way in and said, "Evelyn, keep your coat on. I need you to play the piano for the county jail Christmas Eve service. I think carols would be a good thing."

Evelyn, hoping to find an excuse to stay at the house and share a hot cup of cocoa with her mom, said, "Are you sure there is a piano at the jail?"

"Of course there is a piano at the jail," explained Dad. "I have been leading weekly services there. They asked me to come on Christmas Eve, and the guards said it would be well attended."

"Well, I would think so," Evelyn mumbled under her breath. "Talk about a captive audience."

The next thing she knew, she was thumbing through an old hymnal headed for the county jail in a "less than festive" spirit. But she wasn't surprised: her dad had often taken her to various places in his missionary work.

They arrived at the county jail, where they were searched and escorted down a long hall to the room where the prisoners were waiting. Evelyn was led by a guard to the front of a standing-room-only audience, where she nervously seated herself at the piano. She was the only female in a very crowded room of men.

Relieved to find this jailhouse piano actually in tune, she began to play "Joy to the World." The sound of strong male voices filled the room in one accord. It was surprisingly beautiful. Six or seven carols later, her father began to pray in his deep, strong voice. Evelyn bowed her head and was startled by a tap on her shoulder. It was the guard, requesting her to follow him to a room where the female prisoners were waiting.

Unsure of what to do, she followed the guard down another long hall. The guard said, "No one came to lead a service for the women, and we would like for you to do that." Evelyn quickly began putting together some ideas in her head. She hadn't planned to do this!

A few women, maybe a baker's dozen, were sitting quietly on cold metal chairs arranged in a circle, clearly anticipating that someone would be coming. Evelyn invited them to sing a few Christmas carols with her. After singing "Away in a Manger," one woman spoke up. "That is my son's favorite Christmas carol."

One by one, the women opened up, wanting to talk about their families, their children, and their regrets. Evelyn prayed for each of them, their pasts, their present situations, and their futures. But most of them just wanted Evelyn to pray for their children.

When it was time to leave, they hugged. Evelyn's heart was breaking for them as she headed to her dad's car to return to her warm home and loving family.

Evelyn's dad hadn't planned to give her a "teaching moment." He was just living his Christian life as he always had, and she had been blessed to be part of it.

Every Christmas, there are people who are reborn as children of God. Their past sins are forgiven, their present lives are blessed, and their eternal lives are certain. Jesus became a child so that all people could choose to be reborn and adopted as children of God.

Everyone deserves the chance to truly celebrate Christmas.

THE CHRISTMAS TREE MIRACLE

*"Whoever brings blessing will be enriched,
and one who waters will himself be
watered."*
—PROVERBS 11:25

Sharon spent Christmas of 1960 on Adak, Alaska,
a small island almost at the end of the Aleutian
Islands. Her dad was a career Navy man, and they
had been stationed there for three years. The landing
strip was small, so a ten-seater prop was the largest
plane that could land. Most supplies had to be
carried in on Navy ships.

A few weeks before Christmas, Sharon's dad
informed the family that the ship bringing the
Christmas trees had taken on water. The saltwater
had killed the trees, and it was too late to get more.
The kids were devastated!

What would Christmas be without a tree?

Sharon's mom was a creative person and quickly gathered whatever she could find to make a "replacement tree." Using a dowel rod and red netting, the only color she had, an eighteen-inch tree slowly took shape. The kids all hung small, homemade decorations and put a star on the top. It wasn't the same as a real tree, but it was better than nothing.

On Christmas Eve night, the family heard a commotion outside and music. The kids ran to the door and saw a Navy flatbed truck festooned with Christmas lights coming slowly down the road. The truck soon stopped, and a young serviceman knocked on their door. Sharon's mom opened the door, and the man handed her a small, three-foot tree, calling out, "Merry Christmas!"

Somehow, the Navy had sent trees to them in time for Christmas Day. It was the scrawniest tree Sharon had ever seen, but, as kids, they were elated. Their prayers had been answered. Once decorated, they thought it was the best tree they'd ever had.

Sharon is now seventy years old and still considers that Christmas her most memorable. It's the simplest things in life that are usually the most precious.

Gold, frankincense, and myrrh are often referred to as the gifts in the Christmas story. But the wise men didn't arrive until later. Those are actually the gifts of the "Flight to Egypt" story. However, the biblical Christmas story does include gifts.

Mary and Joseph were gifted with a quiet, private place where she could give birth to her child. The innkeeper didn't have to send his animals away, but he did.

Mary and Joseph were gifted with a visit from the shepherds. Their presence was further encouragement to the young couple that the baby Jesus was the Son of God. Scripture says, "Mary treasured up all these things, pondering them in her heart" (Luke 2:19).

The simple gifts of Christmas are often measured by the kindness of others. They are the memories that we "ponder" years later and "treasure in our hearts." For Sharon, it was a three-foot Christmas tree that arrived on Christmas Eve.

What memory comes to your mind?

More importantly, what memory can you help provide that someone else will treasure?

I wonder about the man who was knocking on the doors of those Navy families. I wouldn't be surprised if one of his lasting Christmas memories was the faces of those excited kids he was able to give a tree to that year.

Treasures are sometimes gold, frankincense, and myrrh. More often, they are like that scrawny, three-foot tree that gave great joy.

WEST TEXAS SNOW

"But as for me and my house, we will serve the Lord."
—JOSHUA 24:15

Susan's home church was First Baptist Abilene, and Dr. Jim Flamming was her preacher. She loved him, and his ministry had led her to accept Christ as her Savior.

Every Christmas Eve, her family attended the 11:00 p.m. evening candlelight service as they anticipated the arrival of Christmas.

On one particular Christmas Eve, her family had their traditional oyster stew and then prepared to go to church. Dr. Flamming brought a message from Luke 1:38, where Mary says, "I am the Lord's servant. May it be to me as you have said."

Susan remembers that the lesson from the pulpit that

night was a simple one: we are all chosen in the way that the Lord will use us. Dr. Flamming taught his church that God calls everyone in a unique way in order to use us for his good purpose.

The simple lesson was years and years ago, but Susan has always remembered it. As her family left the church that night at midnight, after having sung "Silent Night" with only candles glowing, snow gently fell outside. It was a rare treat in Abilene, Texas, but it completed a perfect Christmas Eve. The memory of that night has often inspired Susan's heart and life.

Serving God is an opportunity, but too often we think of it as a chore or duty. God called Mary to an opportunity. She could serve God and provide the world with their Messiah. She said, "Behold, I am the servant of the Lord; let it be to me according to your word" (Luke 1:38). The Lord spared Mary the knowledge of what all those words would mean to her life. The opportunity to serve isn't always easy, but it doesn't change the fact that God called us to be his servants. That calling is our opportunity, not our chore.

Have you ever wondered what might have happened if Mary had refused?

It's easy to imagine why she said yes. It would be difficult to refuse an angel.

Or would it?

God chose a faithful person to carry and give birth to his own Son. God chose a faithful man to join his life with Mary. Joseph had a choice to make too. The Lord calls all of us to himself and gives us the opportunity to serve him with our lives. God doesn't draft workers, but rather asks them to *choose* to serve. He always has.

The Hebrew name for Jesus was *Yeshua*, or Joshua. The Old Testament "Joshua" served the Lord by leading the Hebrew people into the Promised Land. The land had been divided among the families when Joshua called the leaders of those families to make a choice. He said, "Fear the Lord and serve him in sincerity and in faithfulness" (Joshua 24:14).

He reminded them that their ancestors had served other gods while they were in Egypt. Joshua said they would need to "put them away." Joshua told the people to make a choice, saying, "Choose this day whom you will serve, whether the gods your fathers served in the region beyond the River, or the gods of the Amorites in whose land you dwell. But as for me and my house, we will serve the Lord" (v. 15).

It is easy to wear ourselves out by serving the world's holiday expectations. But, there should come a time in each of our holidays when we stand in worship and choose to serve God. Making that choice, over and over again, will be the source of our Christmas blessings.

Servants are the most blessed individuals in Scripture, and the same is true for God's people today.

How will you choose to serve the Lord this Christmas?

AN EXTRAVAGANT GIFT

*"As each has received a gift, use it to serve
one another, as good stewards of God's
varied grace."*
—1 PETER 4:10

Sonya grew up on a farm in Midland, Texas. Every Christmas, her mom would try to make some extra spending money by gathering and selling eggs.

One Christmas, Sonya and her sister had one wish, even though they knew it wouldn't ever happen. Mouton coats were all the rage that year, and only the most fashionable people had one. But they were expensive and considered an *extravagance*. Sonya and her sister knew they could *only* wish.

They had no way of knowing that Sonya's mom had gone to Colberts, the pricey boutique in town, to put those coats on layaway! She wanted her girls to have what they wished for.

One night, while her mom was at a church meeting, the phone rang. Sonya picked it up and heard a saleslady from Colberts say, "The initials for your Mouton coats have arrived." Sonya knew in an instant that the woman on the other end of the line had just "spilled the beans."

Sonya's dad came in from feeding the farm animals, and she told him what had happened. Her dad told her to act like *he was the one* the saleslady had spoken to. But, Sonya's dad wasn't a very good actor. Her mom kept questioning him until he finally had to tell her the truth.

The surprise had been blown, but Sonya and her sister were still thrilled to receive their coats—the coats they had wished for but had never expected to receive.

Most of us can name the gift we *really wanted* but knew we would never receive. Sonya can name that gift and the joy she felt when it was provided. How blessed she and her sister felt to receive those coats, knowing all that it took for her mom to provide them!

Anna was a prophetess who lived at or near the temple in Jerusalem. She was an elderly woman who had become a widow earlier in her life, after only seven years of marriage.

Scripture says, "She did not depart from the temple, worshiping with fasting and prayer night and day" (Luke 2:37). She was at the temple the day Mary and Joseph brought their newborn son. When she saw the baby, the Bible says that "at that very hour she began to give thanks to God and to speak of him to all who were waiting for the redemption of Jerusalem" (Luke 2:38).

Anna had been waiting for the gift of her Messiah for her entire life. She had fasted and prayed, hoping and waiting for the day to come. When Jesus entered the temple, she gave thanks to God and couldn't wait to tell others that their Messiah was born.

Christmas is an important part of God's story, but Easter is as well. Just like Sonya's mom sacrificed to provide her children with a valuable gift, God sacrificed to provide for us: "For God so loved the world" (John 3:16). God so loved the world he gave us *his son.* Then God watched his son give us his life so that we could have our salvation.

Like Anna, we are called to tell others that their Messiah has been born. Will you pray and then watch for the chance to share the news?

Jesus is the most valuable gift that anyone can receive. Who will be grateful to you because they understood what you sacrificed in order to give?

AN UNEXPECTED ARRIVAL

"Now faith is the assurance of things hoped for, the conviction of things not seen."
—HEBREWS 11:1

Bette was only six years old but still remembers her grandmother quickly turning up the little brown radio and then just as quickly turning off the pot of chicken and dumplings simmering on the stove. Still wearing her apron, Grandma grabbed Bette's hand, and they rushed down the wooden porch steps into the street.

They joined all of their neighbors, who were cheering, clapping, singing, and dancing in the street. Horns were honking, flags were waving, and tears were streaming down people's cheeks.

It was 1945 and the war was over.

Two years earlier, Bette and her mom had walked hand in hand to the train station to say goodbye to her daddy. They had family in town. It was a difficult time for Bette's mother, but it was also an important and blessed time.

One day, Bette and her mom were leaving a darkened movie theater when they ran into Bette's best friend from kindergarten. The two girls hugged. The moms introduced themselves. Bette and her friend ran off to play, and the two women found a nearby bench to sit down on.

The women's conversation ended with an invitation for Bette and her mom to accompany her friend's family to church the next Sunday. Bette's mom accepted that invitation. A few weeks later, she accepted Jesus as her Lord. The church had embraced them, knowing they had a loved one fighting overseas.

Bette's dad had gone to church as a young man but had never been discipled. However, on a destroyer in the middle of the Pacific, he prayed on his knees, "God, if you will let me live and get home to my wife and child, I will serve you the rest of my life."

The letters Bette's mom and dad wrote to each other about their commitments to God crossed in the mail somewhere over the ocean.

On December 15, Bette's seventh birthday, she and her mom were sound asleep. They both woke to the knock on the front door. Bette's mom jumped up to answer, and Bette heard the voices. Soon Bette was running into the arms of her daddy, who had come home just in time for Christmas.

Bette wrote, "The war brought out the kindness in others." Bette remembers her mom struggling with her fears, and she remembers watching her mom's faith calm them. Her dad used to say that the war, as awful as it was for so many, had been one of his greatest blessings. They had received their faith. Later, God blessed the family with another "miracle" child and a life of great joy.

Bette will always know that Christmas 1945 was the most important Christmas of her life. Every Christmas after, Bette and her sister would celebrate the holiday with faiths of their own.

For many, this has been a difficult year, but Bette's story puts most of our challenges into a proper perspective. Our earthly lives change, and so do our Christmas seasons. The one consistent foundation to all of life's twists and turns, and every Christmas holiday, is our faith.

Whatever your Christmas will be this year, it will still be the celebration of an "arrival." Whatever blessings we have to celebrate this year, or whatever sorrows we have to mourn, we can always celebrate Christmas with faith in Christ.

THE 3 L'S OF THE ADVENT WREATH

"I came that they may have life, and have it abundantly."
—JOHN 10:10

Taffie was never blessed with children of her own. Nevertheless, Taffie has had hundreds of children, even thousands, during her lifetime. Taffie was a teacher for over forty years.

She taught at several different Christian elementary schools, and Christmas was always a special time of the year for her and her students. Every Christmas, Taffie brought a shiny silver box to school. The other teachers would say, "It must be Advent time because here comes Mrs. O'Conner with her shiny box."

The box contained an Advent wreath that Taffie used each year to teach her students about the meaning of Christmas. She taught them three "L" words using the wreath as her model:

- **Love**: God's love was like the circular shape of the wreath, with no beginning and no end.

- **Life**: The evergreens the wreath was constructed of represented life eternal.

- **Light**: The candles reminded them that Jesus was "the light of the world."

Taffie shared her shiny-box lesson with thousands of children, including the children at the Jewish temple next door. She used the wreath to tell them about Yeshua, who was prophesied in the Old Testament scriptures. She did not have children of her own to raise, but she was blessed to have the opportunity to teach countless children the story of Christmas.

Let's allow Taffie's silver box to be the gift each of us opens this Christmas Day. Inside, you will find God's gifts for you this Christmas.

May your Christmas Day be filled with God's love. Remember 1 John 4:16: "So we have come to know and to believe the love that God has for us. God is love, and whoever abides in love abides in God, and God abides in him." We pray that his perfect love will surround you and that you will feel encircled in his presence all day long.

May your Christmas be a reminder that life on this earth is wonderful, but our best lives still lie ahead. We celebrate Christmas today knowing that one day we will celebrate eternally with Christ.

One day, every day will be a holiday!

And may your Christmas be filled with the light of his life. The skies filled with light when the angels announced Christ's birth. The light of the star led the wise men to their King. Jesus told his disciples, "You are the light of the world" (Matthew 5:14). Then he told them, "Let your light shine before others" (Matthew 5:16). Allow the lights that fill your home today to remind you of the Savior who fills your heart. That light will be your witness to everyone you see today.

This Christmas Day will create memories in your life. I hope you will treasure whatever makes this a special day in your life and the lives of your families.

All of us at Denison Ministries wish you a Merry Christmas and a blessed New Year.

THE DAY AFTER CHRISTMAS

"And we know that for those who love God all things work together for good, for those who are called according to his purpose. For those whom he foreknew he also predestined to be conformed to the image of his Son, in order that he might be the firstborn among many brothers. And those whom he predestined he also called, and those whom he called he also justified, and those whom he justified he also glorified."
—ROMANS 8:28–30

What do you do with all of those Christmas photo cards you receive from family and friends?

Cara wants her boys to keep enjoying them after the holiday season.

After Christmas, she separates the cards into stacks for each of her sons. She turns them into a photo collage and laminates them. Those collages become her son's placemats at the dinner table, and they are encouraged to pick a different friend to pray for each day. It has been a good way to extend the joy of Christmas and the importance of friendship into the new year.

The gift of Christmas is a great reminder that God created us, then saved us, to be a family of faith. Because of Jesus, we have many brothers and sisters in Christ. And because of our Messiah, we were given the opportunity to become children of God.

As the boxes are hauled to the trash, the leftovers are consumed, and you think about the people you know, consider the eternal truth of every Christmas. Jesus was born so that one day people could be born again.

Who needs to become a child of God before next Christmas?

Whom has God placed on your heart to pray for this year?

What special thing can you do that will cause you to pray?

God gave us Christmas so he could give us Easter. Let's live each day as best we can, out of gratitude for those incomparable gifts.

Let's pray for the opportunity to share our story with others so they can share in God's story forever.

Keep writing your story.
Happy New Year!

ABOUT THE AUTHOR

JANET DENISON teaches others to live an authentic faith through her writing, speaking, and teaching ministry.

She blogs weekly at JanetDenison.org and often at ChristianParenting.org. She is also the author of *The Songs Tell the Story* and *Content to Be Good, Called to Be Godly*, among other books.

Janet is the Director of Spiritual Formation for Denison Forum. She also founded ChristianParenting.org in 2015 to equip parents with practical biblical wisdom as they raise children to know and love God.

Janet grew up in California and moved to Texas during her college years. She is a graduate of Houston Baptist University, where she majored in Elementary Education and English. She met her husband at HBU, and they married in 1980.

The Denisons have been privileged to serve four churches: New Hope Baptist Church in Mansfield, Texas; First Baptist Church Midland, Texas; Second-Ponce de Leon Baptist Church in Atlanta, Georgia; and Park Cities Baptist Church in Dallas, Texas.

The Denisons live in Dallas, Texas. When they're not writing or ministering to others, they enjoy spending time with their grown children and their four still-growing grandchildren.

ABOUT DENISON MINISTRIES

DENISON MINISTRIES exists to create culture-changing Christians who are committed to advancing the kingdom through that sphere of influence.

We aspire to influence 3 million Christians every day to experience God through a daily devotional resource (First15.org), to speak into real life through daily cultural commentary (DenisonForum.org), and to bring Jesus into parenting moments (ChristianParenting.org).

NOTES

8 **"Those who walk with God":** Blago Kirov, *Henry Ford: Quotes and Facts* (CreateSpace Independent Publishing Platform, 2016), 4.

33 **"The sacred moments":** Frederick Buechner, *The Magnificent Defeat* (New York: HarperCollins, 1966), 87–88.

34 **"It is not the objective proof of God's existence":** Frederick Buechner, *Secrets in the Dark: A Life in Sermons* (United States: HarperOne, 2009), 19.

41 **"We are the Bibles the world is reading"**: Ann Kannings, *Billy Graham: His Words* (United We are the Bibles the world is reading Kingdom: Lulu.com, 2014).

45 **2.3 billion of us:** Conrad Hackett and David McClendon, "Christians remain world's largest religious group, but they are declining in Europe," Pew Research Center, last modified April 5, 2017, https://www.pewresearch.org/fact-tank/2017/04/05/christians-remain-worlds-largest-religious-group-but-they-are-declining-in-europe/.

45 **Luke interviewed Mary:** Adam C. English, *Christmas: Theological Anticipations* (United Kingdom: Wipf and Stock Publishers, 2016), 56.

Made in the USA
Las Vegas, NV
17 November 2022